THE FOXES

BY
MARK E. AHLSTROM

*The author would like to thank
Peter B. Mohn for his help in
preparing this book.*

EDITED BY
DR. HOWARD SCHROEDER
Professor in Reading and Language Arts
Dept. of Elementary Education
Mankato State University

PRODUCED AND DESIGNED BY
BAKER STREET PRODUCTIONS
Mankato, MN

CRESTWOOD HOUSE
Mankato, Minnesota

CIP

LIBRARY OF CONGRESS CATALOGING IN PUBLICATION DATA

Ahlstrom, Mark E.
  The foxes.

  (Wildlife, habits, and habitat)
  SUMMARY: Describes the physical characteristics, behavior, natural habitat, and relationship to humans of the red and gray foxes.
  1. Foxes—Juvenile literature. [1. Foxes] I. Schroeder, Howard. II. Title. III. Series.
  QL737.C22A34   1983   599.74'442   83-5324
  ISBN 0-89686-220-8

International Standard Book Number:	Library of Congress Catalog Card Number:
Library Binding 0-89686-220-8	83-5324

ILLUSTRATION CREDITS:

National Park Service: Cover, 23
Lynn Rogers: 5, 7, 9, 10, 17, 19, 20, 27, 43
U.S. Forest Service: 15
Sean Morgan/F-Stop: 25
Bob McKeever/Tom Stack & Associates: 28
Gregory A. Yovan/Tom Stack & Associates: 30
G.C. Kelley/Tom Stack & Associates: 33
Mike and Carol Werner/Tom Stack & Associates: 34
Caron Pepper/Tom Stack & Associates: 38
Irene Vandermolen/Tom Stack & Associates: 40
Henry Kartarik: 44

CRESTWOOD HOUSE

Hwy. 66 South, Box 3427
Mankato, MN 56002-3427

86-1481

TABLE OF CONTENTS

INTRODUCTION:

"I had become used to feeding a pair of foxes near the house," Pete wrote from California. "They ate the same kind of dog biscuits I fed my dog. Once in a while they really enjoyed an egg.

"One evening I was waiting for them to appear. As I watched from a window, a large covey of quail flew over the house. This was unusual, because quail rarely fly when they can run away from their enemies. Most of the quail landed on the limbs of a large Bishop pine tree on the other side of the driveway. When the foxes appeared moments later, I knew what had spooked the quail.

"These were gray foxes. They were silver across the back with white bellies. The pair was quite cautious until the female spotted the quail in the tree. As the male watched, she made a rush for the pine and ran up the tree, scattering the quail! She didn't climb like a cat — she actually **ran** up the trunk to the first bunch of limbs. Once on the limbs, she sniffed around for awhile. Then she ran down the trunk, headfirst, to the ground.

"Shortly after that, the foxes discovered their dog biscuits and forgot about the quail.

"I think the foxes became used to me, but they never became real friends," Pete continued. "I've

4

known cautious animals before, but none so cautious as these. Still, they were regular visitors almost every night for more than a year. In the spring, I'm sure I was the first, and maybe the only one, to see the four little fuzzballs. The foxes now had a litter of kits.

"Watching the kits was worth the price of every bit of food I gave them. At first, it seemed they could do nothing but play among themselves. They paid

A gray fox.

5

no attention to my offers of food. As the kits grew, however, they began to eat some of the biscuits. By the end of that summer, the kits were as interested in my treats as their parents.

"There was a benefit in having the foxes around, too. Most of the people around the neighborhood often complained that fall about mice getting into their houses, garages and gardens. I didn't have a one!"

The survivor

The fox is probably one of the smartest wild animals. It is also one of the least understood. The fox is blamed for more mischief in the city and the country than almost any other animal.

People have chased the fox for hundreds of years. Because its fur is thick and rich in color, the fox is hunted and trapped. Its fur is turned into clothing. A common sport in Great Britain and the eastern United States is the foxhunt. The foxhunt consists of a large pack of hounds followed by riders on horses — all chasing after a fox. And farmers sometimes hunt the fox because it kills some of their animals.

So man has not treated the fox too kindly. However, the fox survives, and survives quite well. Some say it survives too well. We shall see about that.
— M.E.A.

CHAPTER ONE

A wild dog

The red fox stood, panting, near the edge of a cliff. The dogs chasing it were closing in. They broke out of the woods and lunged at the fox. At the last moment, the fox stepped to the side. The hounds couldn't stop and fell over the cliff.

Could this happen? Just about everyone who has ever hunted the fox says so.

A red fox.

Whether red fox, gray fox, arctic fox or kit fox, this relative of the wolf and domestic dog is said by many to be the most clever wild animal in North America.

Although the fox is seldom seen, except by hunters and trappers, the fox is found all over the North American continent. Rightly or wrongly, it has been blamed for more problems than just about any other wild animal. The fox has survived the hunter, the trapper, poisons, and other attempts to get rid of it. It has proven that it can take care of itself. This is especially true of the red and gray foxes, which tend to live close to people.

The foxes are the smallest of the wild dogs of North America. Next to a coyote, the largest gray fox would look quite small. The foxes have long, pointed muzzles with small black noses.

But perhaps the most significant feature of the fox is its "brush," or tail. It is a third of the animal's body length. When the fox runs, it holds its tail almost straight out. This makes it look very graceful.

One of the fox's features we seldom see, because few people ever get that close to one, is that its eyes are oval shaped. Other kinds of dogs have round eyes.

Although foxes have lived for up to twelve years in captivity, they seldom live that long in the wild. Most live only until they are four or five years old.

All foxes have large, bushy tails.

A good hunter

Foxes have been at war with farmers for years. Although the fox will eat almost everything, the "fox in the chicken coop" story is the one we hear the most. It has been told by farmers for years. It goes like this:

"Along about dinner time, just after the milking was done, there was a lot of noise in the henhouse. I grabbed my shotgun next to the kitchen door and ran outside. Sure enough, just as I got to the henhouse, out pops this fox with one of my hens in its mouth. I tried to get a shot at it, but it disappeared too quickly. I guess I'll have to put out some poison bait."

Foxes usually hunt only when they are hungry. But that doesn't keep them from killing more than they need to eat. Given the chance, they will kill and store more food for future use. Foxes don't mind eating somewhat spoiled meat, or carrion, as it is called.

A red fox searches for a mouse.

Mice, squirrels, and even insects are food for the fox. They'll eat berries and other fruits, too. The foods it finds in the wild make up most of the fox's diet. Only rarely will it bother a farmer's animals.

The area around a fox's den will show that it isn't particular about its food. There might be bones which once belonged to a deer, feathers from wild birds, the remains of fish and, if you look closely, wings and legs of insects.

It is wrong to assume that the fox caught and killed all those things. The fox is as good at finding leftovers as it is at killing its own food. If another animal, for example, kills a deer and doesn't eat it all, the fox will help itself. The fox, no doubt, is guilty of killing other animals some of the time. But he isn't guilty all of the time.

Like people, the fox is an omnivore. Omnivores eat plant material (like grains and berries) as well as meat. At certain times of the year the fox might eat no meat at all. For example, if there are a lot of ripe berries available, the fox won't have to hunt for animals to eat.

The hunter as the hunted

Unlike the larger wolf, the fox has to be careful of other animals hunting **it**. The fox's small size makes it prey for wild cats, wolves, and coyotes.

A friend told me about an experience he had. He was hunting with some friends in the western part of the United States. They were walking along when all of a sudden they saw two animals break out of some brush. The animals were running like crazy. At first, they thought it was a coyote chasing a rabbit. Then they realized that it was a red fox that the coyote was chasing. The fox was near exhaustion and the coyote quickly caught up. There was a terrible fight, but the coyote won. It killed the fox and carried it off.

The young of the fox, called kits, have their own problems. They are often preyed upon by eagles, hawks and owls. Since the young rarely stray from their parents' side after leaving the den, they are well-protected. But quite often the large birds will get an easy meal.

The worst enemy?

In spite of its natural enemies, the fox's worst enemy may be man. People have chased them for sport and for their fur for hundreds of years.

Early in the development of the United States and Canada, people and foxes seemed to get along fairly well. As cities grew and people moved west, many of the wild animals fled. But not the fox. It began to kill animals that people didn't want to see killed, like farm animals.

When the fox started to be a problem, people decided to do something about it.

In the early 1900's, farmers often held "drives" to kill foxes. A large group of men and boys would walk across the fields hoping to scare up a fox. A fox that got up within shotgun range was as good as dead. Some weekends they might get a hundred foxes, or more.

Another method, used during the 1920's and 1930's, was to hunt them from the air. One person flew the plane and someone else would fly along holding a shotgun. They would try to shoot any fox that they saw from the air.

Years ago bounties were paid to any person who turned in evidence that a fox had been killed. The pelt, or coat, of the fox could then be sold to a fur buyer.

People also used to poison the fox. This was an easy way to kill foxes, and thousands were killed. But there was a problem with this method. Other animals, besides the fox, were killed when they ate the poison meat too.

The fox hunt

In some parts of the country, people sought out the fox in a much different way. This was a method that began in Europe called the foxhunt.

"Tally-ho," cried the master of the hunt. More than fifty foxhounds, all barking loudly, got a whiff of fox scent and broke into a run. Behind the hounds, all dressed in their best riding clothes, rode almost as many people.

A red fox, well-ahead of the hounds had been sighted, and the chase would go on until the dogs caught the fox, or lost its scent. This form of sport still goes on today.

People who do this kind of fox hunting say that it is really an excuse to ride their horses. They feel it is just as much fun even if they never catch a fox.

In fact some fox hunting groups use a "dummy" fox. The dummy, which is a rag soaked in fox scent, is dragged along the ground by a man riding a horse.

A "thing of beauty . . ."

Another threat to the fox has been its fur coat. No matter what color (different types of foxes have coats which are red, gray, black, blue or yellowish),

For years the fox has been trapped for its beautiful fur.

the fox's coat is thick and feels rich. Before the white man came to North America, the Indian trapped foxes for food and clothing. Once the white man moved into the fox range, he also began trapping. But the white men did it for a living. The first foxes were trapped for the European fur market. As North America became more settled, the pelts were sold for use in the United States and Canada.

There are now controlled trapping seasons in most states and provinces. Special rules help insure that too many foxes are not taken.

There are still many trappers that are welcomed by farmers, and trapping provides a living for many people. Good trappers are careful not to take too many foxes. They know that their living depends on a steady supply.

It should be said that none of these efforts to kill the fox have had much lasting effect. Foxes have an amazing ability to survive. Just when people think that all the foxes are gone, more foxes appear.

Disease is fatal

By living so close to civilization, the fox shares some of its problems with man. The biggest problem is disease. Two diseases in particular, rabies and distemper, cause big problems. Both diseases are fatal in wild animals, but domestic animals can be vaccinated against them.

The trouble begins when rabies infects a fox. The rabies can be passed to many different creatures within the area where the fox lives. Skunks, raccoons, opossum, and even family pets that haven't been vaccinated can become infected. Rabid animals seem to go crazy. When the disease is at its peak, the animal may even attack humans. When rabies and distemper attack a fox population, every animal in the area usually dies.

CHAPTER TWO:

Always in motion

The fox is an energetic animal and is always on the move. Of course, the fox finds at least some time to rest. But it must hunt for food every day of the year. The fox searches fields for mice, snakes and insects. It will even leap at low flying birds. It seems most "fond of surprising its prey."

When hunting, the fox likes to surprise its prey.

A friend that lives in the country told about a red fox that was living near his backyard. He also had a gray squirrel which raided his bird feeder almost everyday. The fox and squirrel both knew the other was there. The fox had often tried to catch the squirrel.

One morning, my friend looked out the kitchen window and saw the fox on the ground by a big maple tree. The fox was so still he wondered if it was dead. The squirrel came down the trunk of the tree. About two feet from the ground the squirrel jumped toward his path to the bird feeder. It never made it to the ground. Like a tight spring, the fox jumped and grabbed the squirrel with its mouth.

Raising a family

At around one year of age, the foxes are ready to mate. They begin to pair off in midwinter, during the brief period of time when the female can become pregnant. During this time, the males, called dogs, may fight hard between themselves over the females, called vixens.

After mating, the female seeks out a place to make a den. She might use the same den year after year. Most dens are dug in the ground on the south side of a hill, where the area can be warmed by the sun. The

Two male red foxes fight for the right to mate with a female.

vixen may also move into a burrow made by another animal. She will rebuild it to her liking. Gray foxes may nest in hollow trees.

A fox's den is fairly easy to spot. Worn trails will lead to it. Parts of things the fox didn't eat, like bones and feathers, will be around the opening to the den. The den may even have a bad odor.

That's only the main entrance, however. To escape from its enemies, the vixen may dig other tunnels. Some of the tunnels may be seventy-five feet (23 m) long, with many areas for food storage.

Slightly more than eight weeks after mating, the young, called kits, are born. Four kits is the average litter for all types of foxes. Litters of eight, nine, and ten have been reported.

When the kits are born they weigh two-and-a-half to four ounces (70-115 gm). The kits' eyes open after about ten days.

The opening to a red fox's den.

During the first few weeks after the kits are born, the male does all the hunting. He brings food to the opening of the den for the vixen. The female spends all of her time with the kits, nursing and cleaning them.

In three to four weeks the kits can be seen near the opening of the den. Still nursing, they begin to make short trips. The kits don't go far from the den, and usually both parents go along.

At an age of eight to ten weeks the vixen forces the kits to quit nursing. Now they must hunt for their food. All through the late spring, summer and early autumn, the kits hunt with their parents. They are slowly learning how to get food. By autumn the kits will be able to survive on their own. In the late autumn the "family" breaks up. Nature has decided that their chances of surviving are better if they live apart. The foxes now live alone until the winter breeding season.

Many kinds of foxes

There are four main types of foxes in North America — the red, the gray, the arctic, and the kit. Many things about them are similiar, but there are many interesting differences. We'll now take a look at them.

CHAPTER THREE

Reynard

In Europe, the red fox *(Vulpes fulva)* is known as Reynard. It's a title of respect. The red fox is very clever and has found many ways to avoid being caught by its enemies.

In the United States, the red fox is found in every state but Florida. Its range extends across Canada almost to the treeless tundra of the Arctic. It lives in the mountains, in forests and on farmlands. The fox has adapted to the severe winter cold of the North, but lives just as well in the warm areas of the South.

The red fox is usually around fifteen inches (38 cm) tall at the shoulder. It weighs between eight and fourteen pounds (3.6-6.4 kg). Including its tail, it is usually between thirty-six and forty inches (92-103 cm) long.

Not all red foxes are red. Some of them have black fur, and some have fur that is red and black mixed. Usually the fur on the belly is white. On a red fox the tip of the tail will always be white. Except for the arctic fox, which can be all white in winter, the red fox is the only fox to have a white tip on its tail.

This red fox from Alaska is almost all black.

A clever animal

The legends about the red fox are many. Most of them have to do with its cleverness. Some American Indians who noticed its tricks thought it was the devil on earth. History books tell of the time a hundred white men formed a posse to catch red foxes that had been killing chickens. Two men, it is said, were shot by accident. All foxes escaped!

An expert on wildlife explained more about how clever a red fox can be. He was watching a pair of foxes. The female was taking care of the kits. The male was trying to find a field mouse in a burrow nearby. Suddenly, he heard a dog bark nearby. The male fox gave up his hunt and ran back to the female and the kits. They all went into their den.

In a short time, the male came out and ran toward the dog. He stopped at least three times and urinated to leave his scent. Then he ran several circles around the area and left.

The expert climbed a tree for a better view. He could see the fox running away to his left. The fox was zig-zagging all over the place. Twice the fox stopped still, then jumped as far as it could. The first time he jumped to the left of the trail. The second time he jumped way to the right. A short time later the dogs — there were three — hit the trail the fox had left near the den. The dogs spent a good five minutes running and sniffing around the area. Finally, one of the dogs found a strong scent. Then all three of the dogs took off after the fox.

The expert decided to wait and see what would happen next.

About three hours later the male fox returned. The observer waited until it was dark to see if the dogs would come back. They never did.

Because the expert knew who owned the dogs, the next day he checked with the owner. The owner told him that the first of his dogs finally got home about nine in the evening. The second got home awhile later. The third hadn't come home yet! The fox had tricked the dogs!

The red fox has many other ways to escape danger.

To avoid leaving its scent, an escaping red fox might walk down the top of a fence to put distance between his last foot track and the next. Or it might run many feet down the middle of a stream. One

To avoid leaving its scent for a predator to follow, the red fox will walk in a stream.

such fox, having run down a stream, came back and hid under a bridge as hunters walked across it! When hounds and hunters were gone, the fox came out. It shook the water off its coat, and trotted off in the other direction.

There's another story about the red fox. A lot of farmers believe that a fox will wander away from his "home" area to kill chickens. That way, if the owner of those chickens gets upset, he'll go after the fox that lives closet to his henhouse, and not the actual thief.

Because the odds seem to be so much in its favor, it seems that the red fox enjoys being chased.

The "silver" fox

Every so often, a pair of red foxes will produce a kit with a silvery coat. The fur of this rare red fox is prized by those who make and buy fur coats.

Some people have tried to capture wild red foxes and breed the silver fox in captivity. It may or may not work, even when the foxes are taken as kits. Nothing is going to force wild creatures to do something against their nature. Most attempts have ended in failure.

CHAPTER FOUR:

The tree fox

The gray fox *(Urocyon cinereoargenteus)* has a smaller range across North America than the red fox. The two types do share certain parts of their ranges, however. The gray fox tends to avoid areas that have very cold winter weather, but it does exist in parts of southern North America that the red fox seems to avoid. The gray fox likes to live in wooded areas.

This gray fox stretches after taking a nap.

It is not found in the plains states or the north-western mountain states of the United States. The gray fox is found everywhere else in the United States, however. A few cross over into southeastern Canada and Central America. Gray foxes are found all over Mexico.

One of the gray fox's nicknames is "tree fox," since it often climbs up leaning trees. It likes to take a nap on the low branches. Gray foxes have been seen in trees eating eggs or young birds out of their nests.

The gray fox will also climb trees to escape its

The gray fox climbs trees to hunt and to escape predators.

enemies. Usually they will climb out on a leafy branch and flatten themselves against it. It takes a sharp eye to spot them. Gray foxes will use this trick when they are chased by dogs.

The gray fox is less ready to live near humans than the red fox. People are also less likely to see the gray fox because it moves around mostly at night.

The fur on the gray fox's back usually is a silver-gray; but it can have orange, black, and white markings. The foxes belly can be either white or light gray. To tell it apart from the kit foxes, you have to check the tail. On a gray fox the tip of the tail is either dark gray, or black, and it has a line of very dark guard hairs that run from the tip to the base of the tail. (Guard hairs are long hairs that stick out of the fur.) The kit fox doesn't have guard hairs.

The gray fox weighs less than the red fox, but it is longer. Fully-grown gray foxes are between thirty-two and forty-five inches (82-115 cm) long. They will weigh between seven and eleven pounds (3.1-5 kg). The gray fox can be up to fifteen inches (38 cm) tall at the shoulder.

A fierce fighter

Generally gray foxes are the best fighters of all the foxes. Many domestic dogs have found this out the hard way. A gray fox has no trouble defending itself

The gray fox usually won't avoid a fight. In this case, the fox decided to take on the photographer.

from a single dog. If a dog threatens a gray fox, its mate, or its kits it will be easily driven away.

Fierce fights often occur between the males before the mating of gray foxes begins. Rarely do they kill one another, but almost all male foxes older than a year or two carry some scars of battle. Torn ears and scars on the muzzle are most frequent.

This habit of fighting also shows itself during the mating ritual. Pete, the friend from California mentioned in the Introduction, saw this ritual during the third week in January. If he hadn't heard the noise, he wouldn't have known anything was going on.

It was early evening so Pete switched on the yard lights and looked out the window. In a clearing were two gray foxes. They were standing with their heads lowered and seemed to be glaring at each other. One of the foxes, it turned out to be the male, took a step forward, very carefully. Then "snap!" The female acted like she wanted to bite the male's nose off. She bared her fangs and growled. It was a funny growl, because it was so high-pitched. The male backed off and she chased him.

My friend was about to turn the outside lights off, when the female came back to the clearing and "yapped." The male wasn't far away because he came back within seconds. No matter what the male tried, the vixen snapped at him and chased him. This happened a dozen times in the next ninety minutes. Finally both foxes left.

Fifty-five days later, the vixen stopped showing up for the dog biscuits my friend gave them. About four weeks later, when she did show up, she and the male had four kits with them!

Around the den

The female usually builds her den in a hollow log lying on the ground, or in a hollow tree. If no hollow logs or trees are available, the female will dig out a den in the ground like other foxes.

Outside the den you are likely to find everything from bird bones to fish bones. You might also find bits and pieces of rabbit fur, along with a couple of skulls. The skulls could have come from a dog, another fox, or maybe a small raccoon. Just like other foxes, grays may be great hunters, but they are sloppy housekeepers!

The gray fox is neither hunted nor trapped as much as the red. This is because it doesn't bother people as much. It's more likely to do its hunting in the wild than in the henhouse. And its fur is not desired as much by the fur-wearing public.

CHAPTER FIVE:

The small fox

The kit fox *(Vulpes velox),* and several related foxes that live in desert and plains areas, are the smallest of all the foxes. They also have the smallest range in which to live. The kit fox is found in parts of California, Oregon, Nevada, Utah, Arizona, Montana, Colorado, Wyoming, New Mexico and Texas

The kit fox is the smallest of the foxes.

in the United States. It lives in small parts of Saskatchewan and Alberta in Canada. They are also found in small areas of northern Mexico. The kit fox prefers dry, brushy areas.

Because of its speed, and its habit of darting after things, the kit fox is sometimes called the swift fox. It's hardly bigger than a large house cat. These foxes have yellow-gray coats, black-tipped tails, and lighter colored bellies. Adult kit foxes weigh between four and six pounds (1.8-2.7 kg). Including their tails, they are between twenty-four and thirty-two inches (62-82 cm) long, most of them are about twelve inches (31 cm) tall at the shoulder.

Kit foxes have very long ears.

The kit fox is rarely seen in the daytime. It spends most of its time during the day in a burrow in the ground. Game managers say the kit fox almost always prefers to take over a burrow already made by another burrowing animal. However, it remakes the burrow to satisfy its own needs. If, for example, the burrow doesn't have a second entrance, the kit fox will make one. The second entrance is made because foxes of all kinds always want several ways to escape enemies.

Most foxes, when surprised, will run. The kit may freeze instead, hugging the ground. The color of the kit's fur allows it to blend in with its desert surroundings. When chased, the kit relies more upon speed than cleverness. This is caused by the fact that in desert areas there are not too many places to hide.

Because it would waste energy by hunting during the heat of the day, the kit fox feeds at night. Ground squirrels, prairie dogs, rabbits, snakes, lizards, small birds and insects are all part of the kit's diet. It finds itself attacking animals almost as large as itself, like rabbits, at times. If a kit fox goes several days without finding an animal to eat, it may eat grass and berries.

The kit fox has a "voice" unlike other foxes. Instead of yelping and yapping like other foxes, it chatters much like a squirrel. And the kit fox's ears are very long in relation to the size of its body. It has the longest ears of all the foxes.

The kit fox may mate a little earlier in the southern part of its range than the kit foxes in the northern part, but the results are almost always the same. A litter of four or five little ones arrives in late spring. Like all other foxes, the family breaks up when the young mature in the fall.

Another closely related relative of the kit called the desert fox is found in the kit's range. The desert fox lives in both the desert and the nearby prairie areas. The two are almost identical. It would take an expert to tell them apart.

People and kit foxes don't mix

As people have tried to kill coyotes and other predators across the range of the kit fox, the kit also has suffered. Even though it is too small to be able to kill farmer's livestock, many kit foxes have been killed when they ate poisoned bait that had been put out for coyotes.

People have also affected the kit fox in another way. Unlike red and gray foxes, which have adapted to living near people, the kit fox can't. As desert areas are irrigated and made into farmlands, the kit fox has to move on. The main reason is that the animals that the kit fox feeds on live only in desert areas. Without this food the kit fox cannot survive.

CHAPTER SIX:

The white fox

The artic fox *(Alopex lagopus)* is the least like the other foxes that live in North America. It has a shorter nose, and short, rounded ears.

Unlike the other foxes, its build is rather stocky. It usually is not over thirty-six inches (92 cm) in length, and seldom grows over twelve inches (31 cm) tall at the shoulder. And yet it can weigh as much as fifteen pounds (6.8 kg). This makes it the heaviest of the foxes.

The arctic fox does something else that makes it unusual. It changes colors with the seasons. During the summer months it is gray-brown on its back and white on its belly. In the winter it is white all over. This color change, called molting, is nature's way of giving camouflage to the artic fox. The color change happens in response to the changing habitat of the area this fox lives in.

The home of the artic fox is the treeless tundra of the Arctic area of North America. In winter this area is covered with snow and ice. The fox's white coat makes it all but invisible during this time. As the snow melts in the spring, exposing the ground, the

37

The arctic fox lives on the treeless tundra of the Arctic.

color of the artic fox changes. It sheds its white fur and grows gray-brown fur on its back. Once again the fox blends in with its surroundings.

Living on leftovers

In the winter, the arctic fox lives mostly on leftovers. The fox will often follow a wolf pack, eating whatever the wolves leave behind.

Other arctic foxes may search the edges of the sea, where polar bears may leave bits and pieces of seals that they have killed. The fox will wait until the bears have eaten their fill and moved on. Then the fox will get its dinner.

Should a whale strand itself on shore, the arctic fox may not have to search for food for a long time.

In the summer, the arctic fox hunts mainly for lemmings and other rodents. It may also eat birds like the ptarmigan (a bird which resembles a grouse), and bird eggs.

No other fox seems to have to travel so far to feed as the arctic fox. When one of its main meals of the summer, the lemming, is scarce, it may range far to the south in search of food. In the winter these foxes also have been seen well away from land foraging on the pack ice that covers the ocean.

The arctic fox gets along with man much better than the other types of foxes. Alaskan and Canadian explorers and trappers say this fox often follows them on their journeys. They seem to have learned that it is a good way to get an easy meal.

The arctic fox has the smallest ears of all the foxes.

Raising the kits

Kits are usually born in hillside dens late in the spring. Until they begin to mature, they wear brown coats. Like the adults they lose their brown coats at the end of the summer, and grow a new white one.

Training of the kits occurs in much the same way as the kits of other foxes. At first, the kits just go along with their parents on hunting trips. They learn to hunt by watching what the adult foxes do to catch their prey. After awhile they start to catch food for themselves. By the time autumn arrives, the kits will be able to survive on their own.

Beautiful fur

Of all the fox family, the arctic fox may have the most beautiful pelt. Not only is it the softest of all fox pelts, but people like the white color. Thousands of arctic foxes are trapped every winter when their coats are at their best. Trapping the fox is a major industry for the Eskimos.

There is one type of arctic fox that is especially valued for its fur. Sometimes the arctic fox will have a smoky-blue coat instead of a white one. This blue phase may occur anywhere within their range, or even within the same litter. They are most commonly found in Iceland and on the Pribilof Islands off the Alaskan coast.

Since the arctic fox lives and breeds not just in the Alaskan and Canadian arctic, but in Iceland and other arctic areas, there seems to always be plenty of them. Some of the areas are so hard to get to that the arctic fox is never bothered at all. So trapping is not much of a threat to the survival of the arctic fox.

CHAPTER SEVEN

Fox watching

How does one go about seeing a fox?

The best way to start is to ask your area wildlife officer what area might have foxes. Then go there. But don't be disappointed if you don't see a fox. They are clever, remember.

One way of finding foxes to begin with is to find the fox's den, especially during the spring denning season. At that time, when the kits are young, there's plenty of travel from the den to the hunting areas. You may find trails leading to and from the den. Den openings will have their own rather bad odor. You may be able to smell them from a long way off. If a den is found, the watcher should hide in an area away from the trails the fox has made.

Unless you're very lucky, you will need binoculars. It also helps to have a blind, or a shelter you can hide behind, so you can see the fox but it can't see you. Find a comfortable position and be ready to move very slowly if you see something. Be very patient.

City, county, state and national parks may offer good chances. There, all wildlife is probably protected. Without hunting pressure, the sly fox may have a chance to relax. and allow itself to be seen.

There is one very important rule to follow. If you run into a fox which seems friendly, get out of there in a hurry. And never let your family pets come into contact with it. A fox that doesn't run away when it sees you is most likely a sick one. It might have rabies. If anything, you want to get away from the animal, not closer.

It takes patience to spot a fox in the wild.

The future

The fox is still considered a predator throughout most of the country. That's fair, because it is a predator. If game managers have learned anything in this century, it is that predators aren't all that bad. When foxes kill too many of their prey, they suffer as much, if not more than, the prey. Soon they have no food and may starve. And predators serve a purpose by controlling the numbers of such animals as rats and mice. It's all a part of the natural system of nature that is finally being recognized.

Reynard, the "devil on earth," has made it through centuries of being hunted, poisoned and trapped. It has survived its own diseases. It's still around in big numbers and probably will be for a long time to come.

A red fox hunts along the edge of a field.

GLOSSARY:

BIOLOGIST - A person who is an expert on all living things.

CAMOUFLAGE - Coloring that allows a person or animal to hide.

CARRION - Dead or rotting meat.

DOG - A male fox.

FORAGE - To look for food.

KIT - A baby fox.

MOLTING - To shed hair or feathers.

OMNIVORE - An animal that eats both meat and plants.

PREDATOR - An animal that hunts and eats other animals (called prey).

PREY - An animal that is hunted and eaten by another animal (called a predator).

RANGE - The area an animal naturally lives in, that provides food and shelter.

VACCINATE - An injection, or shot, that protects against disease.

VIXEN - A female fox.

Red and Kit Foxes

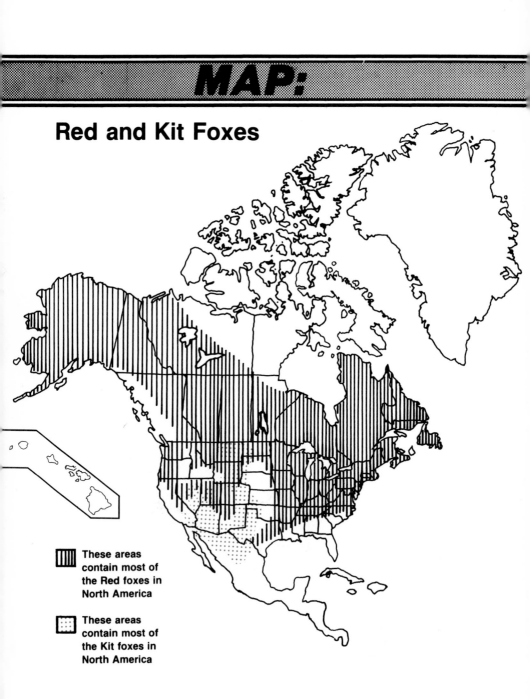

▐▌▐▌ These areas
contain most of
the **Red** foxes in
North America

▦ These areas
contain most of
the **Kit** foxes in
North America

46

Gray and Arctic Foxes

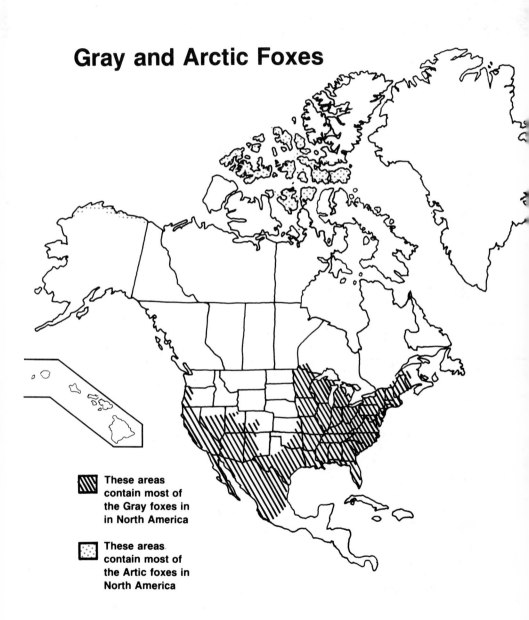

These areas contain most of the Gray foxes in in North America

These areas contain most of the Artic foxes in North America

WILDLIFE
HABITS & HABITAT

READ AND ENJOY THE SERIES:

THE **WHITETAIL** • THE **PHEASANT**

THE **BALD EAGLE** • THE **WOLVES**

THE **SQUIRRELS** • THE **BEAVER**

THE **GRIZZLY** • THE **MALLARD**

THE **RACCOON** • THE **WILD CATS**

THE **RATTLESNAKE** • THE **SHEEP**

THE **ALLIGATOR** • THE **CARIBOU**

THE **CANADA GOOSE** • THE **FOXES**